Life in a S

Contents

Creatures in Shells

Some creatures have shells. Shells provide protection. Shells can be homes, too.

3

Snails

A snail has a shell on its back. When there is danger, the snail can pull its whole body inside its shell. Snails also do this when the weather is very hot or very cold.

Sea snail

Do You Know?

As a snail grows, its shell grows bigger, too.

5

Turtles and Tortoises

A turtle has a shell on its back and under its body. When there is danger, a turtle can pull its head and legs inside its shell.

Do You Know?

A tortoise is a kind of turtle. Tortoises live on the land.

Do You Know?

Turtles and tortoises have patterns on their shells. No two shells have exactly the same pattern.

Turtles

Tortoises

7

Crabs and Lobsters

Lobsters have shells that cover them all over. So do most crabs.

Crab

Do You Know?

The shell of a crab or a lobster is called an exoskeleton. This means it is a skeleton outside the creature's body.

Lobster

9

Hermit Crabs

A hermit crab has a shell on its legs and claws, but not on its body. To protect its soft body, it lives inside another creature's shell. When the hermit crab grows bigger, it moves to a bigger shell.

This hermit crab is living in an empty shell
that once belonged to a sea snail.

Open and Shut

Some shellfish, such as clams, have shells that can open and shut. When the creature inside is in danger, it can snap its shell shut!

Do You Know?

Sea otters eat shellfish. They use a rock to open the shell.

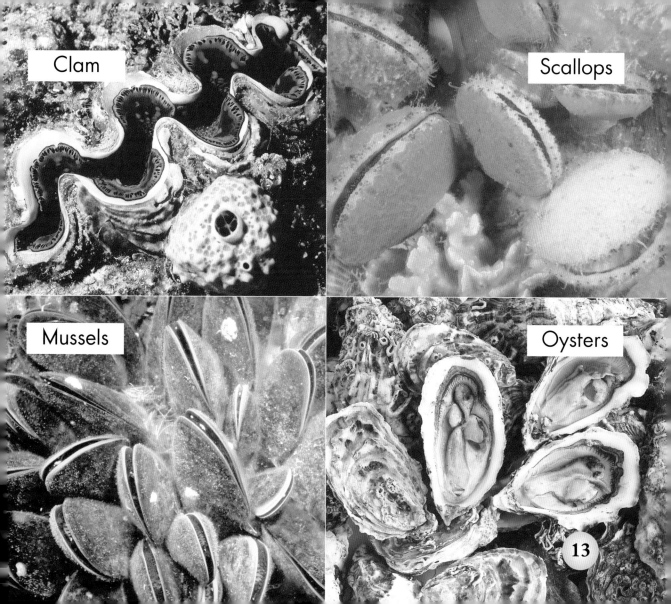

Clam

Scallops

Mussels

Oysters

13

At the Beach

Sometimes shells that are very near the sea still have a creature living inside them. The creature in the shell needs to be covered by seawater for several hours a day. This happens when the tide comes in.

NOTICE

Do not take shells from this beach. Living creatures may still be inside!

15

Index